Mountains

KINGFISHER

Kingfisher Publications Plc
New Penderel House
283–288 High Holborn
London WC1V 7HZ
www.kingfisherpub.com

First published by Kingfisher Publications Plc 2007
2 4 6 8 10 9 7 5 3 1
1TR/1106/PROSP/RNB/140MA/F

ISBN 978 07534 1378 4

Senior editor: Belinda Weber
Designer: Rebecca Johns
Cover designer: Poppy Jenkins
Picture research manager: Cee Weston-Baker
DTP co-ordinator: Catherine Hibbert
Production controller: Jessamy Oldfield
Indexer: Hilary Bird

Printed in China

Acknowledgements
The publishers would like to thank the following for permission to reproduce their material. Every care has been taken
to trace copyright holders. However, if there have been unintentional omissions or failure to trace copyright holders,
we apologize and will, if informed, endeavour to make corrections in any future edition.
b = bottom, *c* = centre, *l* = left, *t* = top, *r* = right

Photographs: *cover* Getty Stone; 1 Corbis/W Wayne Lockwood; 2–3 Corbis/Charlie Munsey; 4–5 Alamy/Nagelestock; 6–7 Corbis/Eye
Ubiquitous; 7*tr* Corbis/Galen Rowell; 9 Corbis/Reuters; 10–11 Photolibrary.com; 11*br* Getty/Science Faction; 12 Corbis/Joseph Sohm;
13 Corbis/Ric Ergenbright; 15*tr* Frank Lane Picture Agency/Winfried Wisniewski; 15*bl* Arboretum de Villardebelle, France; 16–17 Getty/
Stone; 17*br* Alamy/Aflo Foto; 18*l* Corbis/Galen Rowell; 18–19 Getty/Imagebank; 19*r* Photolibrary.com; 20 Corbis/Eye Ubiquitous;
21*t* Corbis/Tom Bean; 21*br* Corbis/Paul A Souders; 22 Alamy/Brett Baunton; 23*t* Natural History Picture Agency/Alberto Nardi;
23*b* Science Photo Library/Kaj R Svensson; 24 Corbis/Steve Kaufman; 25*t* Alamy/Imagina Photography; 25*b* Corbis/Joe McDonald;
26*c* Alamy/Andrew Woodley; 26–27*b* Getty/Stone; 27*t* Alamy/Terry Fincher Photos; 28–29 Photolibrary.com; 29*t* Alamy/Mediacolor's;
30 Corbis/Zefa; 31*t* Getty/Photographer's Choice; 31*br* Getty/Aurora; 32 Getty/Digital Vision; 33*tl* Alamy/David R Frazier Photolibrary;
33*b* Alamy/Phototake; 34 Alamy/Publiphoto Diffusion; 35*tl* John Cleare Mountain Camera; 35*b* Getty/Photographer's Choice;
36*c* Royal Geographical Society; 36*br* Corbis Montagne Magazine; 37 Corbis/Sygma; 38 Alamy/f1 online; 38–39 Alamy/StockShot;
39*c* Corbis/Ashley Cooper; 40 Corbis/EPA; 41*t* Corbis/John van Hasselt; 41*b* Frank Lane Picture Agency/Foto Natura;
43*tl* Getty/NGS; 43*b* Mary Evans Picture Library; 48 Alamy/Imagestate

Illustrations on pages: 8, 11, 12, 13, 16 Peter Winfield; 14–15 Steve Weston

Commissioned photography on pages 44–47 by Andy Crawford
Project-maker and photoshoot co-ordinator: Jane Thomas
Thank you to models Jamie Chang-Leng, Mary Conquest and Georgina Page

 Kingfisher Young Knowledge

Mountains

Margaret Hynes

Contents

What are mountains? 6

Moving world 8

Mountains of fire 10

Rising rock 12

On the mountainside 14

Mountain weather 16

Glaciers 18

Wear and tear 20

Plucky plants 22

Adaptable animals 24

Living on mountains 26

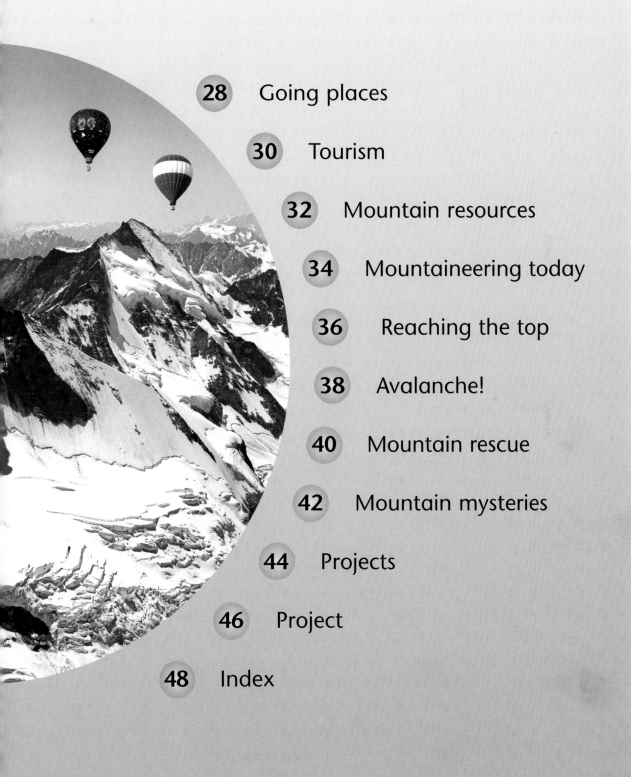

28 Going places

30 Tourism

32 Mountain resources

34 Mountaineering today

36 Reaching the top

38 Avalanche!

40 Mountain rescue

42 Mountain mysteries

44 Projects

46 Project

48 Index

What are mountains?

A mountain is a giant, steep-sided rock that rises above the earth's surface. There are mountains on land, under the oceans and even on other planets.

Mighty mountain ranges

A group of mountains is called a range. The Himalayas is a mountain range in Asia. It is home to the world's highest peaks.

peaks – the top parts of a mountain

Cold at the top

There is less, or thinner, air at the top of a mountain than there is at the bottom. It is also colder, so some peaks are snowy all year.

air – *the mixture of gases we breathe*

Moving world

The earth's rocky surface is called the crust. It is divided into plates, which fit together like a jigsaw. The plates move very slowly over the face of the earth.

Moving plates

This map shows the plates and the direction they are moving in. Some plates crash into each other while others pull apart.

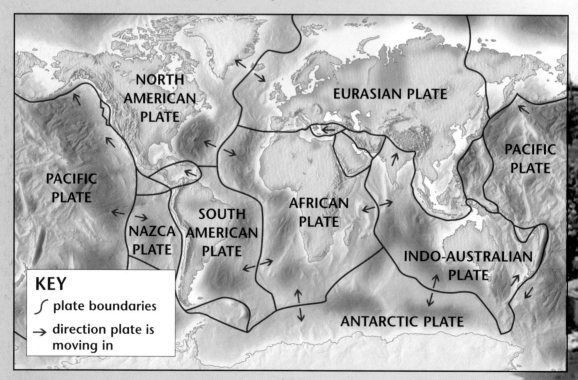

NORTH AMERICAN PLATE

EURASIAN PLATE

PACIFIC PLATE

PACIFIC PLATE

NAZCA PLATE

SOUTH AMERICAN PLATE

AFRICAN PLATE

INDO-AUSTRALIAN PLATE

ANTARCTIC PLATE

KEY

∫ plate boundaries

→ direction plate is moving in

plates – large areas of land that 'float' on the liquid rock underneath

Earthquakes

When the edges of two plates grip each other, the plates cannot move. If they shift suddenly, an earthquake happens, causing terrible damage.

crust – *the hard, rocky surface of the earth*

Mountains of fire

Some mountains are volcanoes. They form when hot, melted rock, called magma, erupts from a crack in the earth's crust. The liquid rock cools and hardens into a mountain.

Violent eruption

Mount Etna is a volcano in Italy. When it erupts, magma bursts out. Ash, gas, steam and hot rocks shoot into the sky.

erupts – explodes, throwing ash, gas and hot rocks into the air

Hotspots

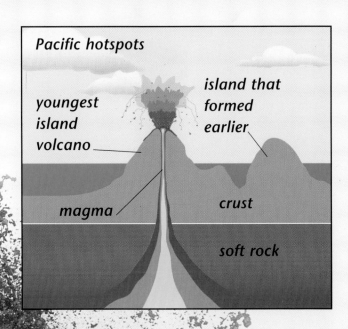

Pacific hotspots

youngest island volcano

island that formed earlier

magma

crust

soft rock

The Hawaiian islands are volcanoes. They form as the Pacific plate passes over a hot and active area called a hotspot.

Flowing lava

Once magma pours out of a volcano it is called lava. It rolls downhill, like a river of fire.

lava – melted rock on the earth's surface

Rising rock

Many mountains form in areas where plates push against each other. The moving plates squeeze the land up, creating mountains.

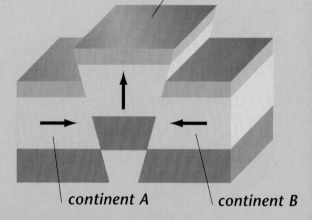

squeezing action pushes up blocks of rock

continent A   *continent B*

Fault-block mountains

The moving plates can cause cracks in the crust. These break the crust into blocks and some rise up to form fault-block mountains.

Rounded off

The Wasatch range in Utah, USA, is a fault-block mountain range. Its blocky shape has been worn down over time.

fault – a crack in the earth's crust

Fold mountains

When two plates crash together, they can cause layers of rock in the crust to buckle and rise. This forms fold mountains.

valley

mountain

continent A crashes into continent B

continent B

Folding rock

As the layers of rock in the crust are squashed, they form zigzagging shapes called folds.

buckle – *to crumple and fold*

A high mountain has several zones, or regions. Each zone has different plants and animals. Very few plants or animals live near the top.

conifers

Plant cover

Forests cover the mountain's lower region. Further up is a zone of small, low-lying plants called alpines.

deciduous trees

icy peak

alpine region

Mountain birds

The wind is so strong at the top of mountains that only powerful birds, such as this lammergeier, can fly there.

Conifers

These cones and pine needles belong to the spruce conifer. Conifer trees have a triangular shape. This helps the snow slide off them.

deciduous trees – *trees that lose their leaves in autumn*

Mountain **weather**

The weather can change very quickly on mountains. A storm can start in just a few minutes. The temperature can quickly drop to below freezing.

Rain shelter

Some mountains are so high they block rain clouds. One slope may be rainy while the other side stays dry.

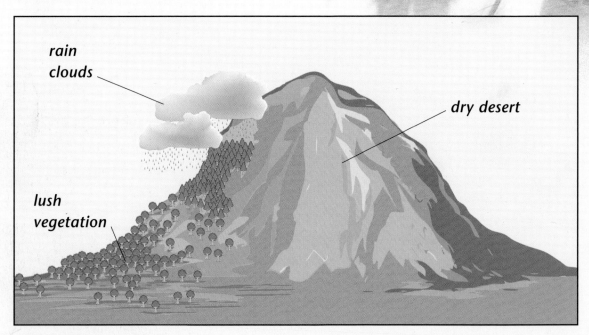

rain clouds

dry desert

lush vegetation

***vegetation** – plant life*

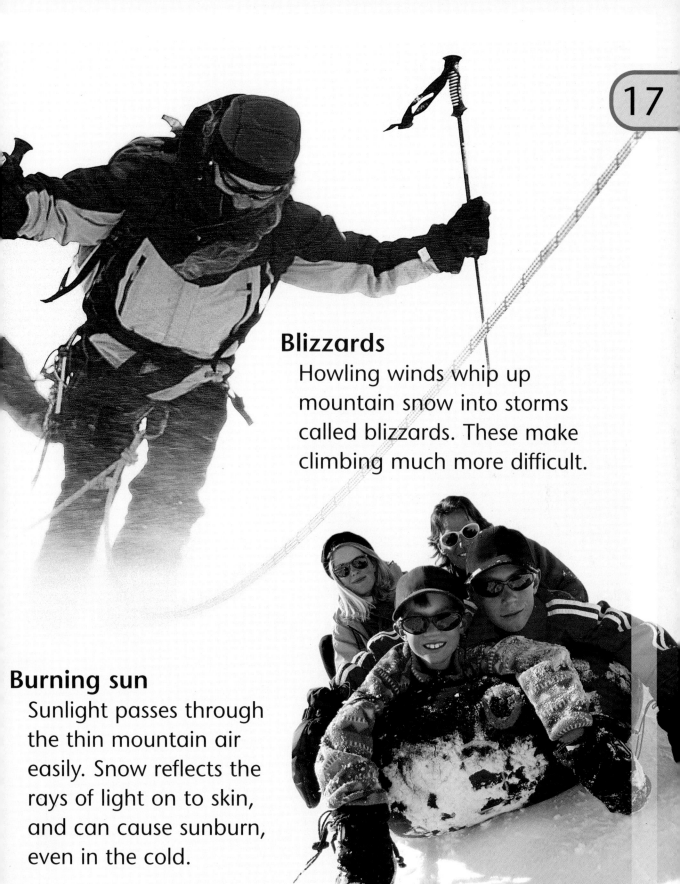

Blizzards

Howling winds whip up mountain snow into storms called blizzards. These make climbing much more difficult.

Burning sun

Sunlight passes through the thin mountain air easily. Snow reflects the rays of light on to skin, and can cause sunburn, even in the cold.

reflects – when light rays bounce back from the surface

Glaciers

Great rivers of ice, called glaciers, form on the peaks of some of the world's highest mountains. The glaciers move downhill very slowly.

How glaciers form

Snow collects in rocky hollows, called cirques, high up the mountain. The snow turns into ice, and forms a glacier.

hollows – *shallow holes*

Cracks in the ice

Cracks, called crevasses, form in a glacier as it moves over bumpy ground. They are very deep and dangerous so climbers use safety ropes.

Left behind

Glaciers pick up rubble and drag it along with them. When the ice melts, these rocks are left behind.

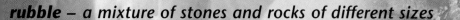

rubble – a mixture of stones and rocks of different sizes

Wear and tear

All mountains are under attack from the elements. Ice, wind and running water slowly wear them down over millions of years.

Old mountain

A young mountain is jagged. As it gets older, the elements slowly wear it down and it becomes more rounded.

elements – the group name for earth, fire, air and water

Ice sculptures

As a glacier creeps along,
it scrapes at the mountainside.
Eventually it gouges out huge
U-shaped valleys, such as this
one in California, USA.

Rolling rocks

Ice chisels away small
rocks from the mountain.
These tumble down the
slope and gather in
a heap at the bottom.

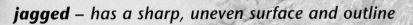

jagged – *has a sharp, uneven surface and outline*

Plucky plants

Plants that grow high up on the mountain slopes have adapted to cope with the biting cold, fierce winds and freezing weather there.

Tiny trees

Some willow and birch trees grow high up the mountainside. They avoid the howling winds by hugging the ground.

Alpine snowbell

The alpine snowbell gives off heat, which melts the snow around it. The plant's heat enables it to bloom in spring.

Growing on rocks

Lichens live on rocky peaks. They make acids that make the rocks crumble. Then they send tiny roots into the rocks to suck up any goodness in them.

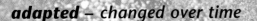

adapted – changed over time

Adaptable animals

Some animals that live on mountains have adapted to cope with the steep slopes. Others have adapted to living with high winds and freezing conditions.

Hot bath

Japanese macaque monkeys wallow in hot pools during the cold winters. The water is heated by volcanoes.

suction – the ability to suck a surface and stick to it

Mountain climber

Mountain goats are good at scrabbling over the rocky mountain faces. Their hooves are hollow and act like suction pads, helping the goats grip.

Natural anti-freeze

The Yarrow's spiny lizard's blood stays liquid in temperatures below freezing, so it can survive on icy peaks in Mexico.

anti-freeze – a substance that prevents things from freezing

Living on **mountains**

Mountain peoples have learned to live in steep, remote and sometimes dangerous places. They grow crops for food and raise animals there.

Mountain animals

Yaks are useful animals. They provide food and wool to farmers. They are also used to carry goods.

facilities – buildings and services, such as health care and schools

Mountain cities

Kathmandu nestles in the Himalayas. It has the same facilities as any other modern city.

Growing food

Mountain fields are steep and there is not much soil. Many farmers build terraces to stop the soil washing away.

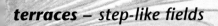

terraces – step-like fields

Going places

It can be difficult to travel on mountains because they are very steep. People have come up with clever ways for making mountain travel easier.

Long and winding roads

Mountain roads do not follow a straight line because they would be too steep to climb. The roads take a zigzagging route instead.

zigzagging – *twisting and turning*

Climbing on a cable

A moving cable pulls this cable car between stations at the top and bottom of a mountain. Skiers use cable cars to get to snow high up on mountains.

cable – *a long, thick rope usually made from metal wire*

Tourism

Mountains are great places to explore and enjoy. People can ski, trek, climb or mountain bike along the steep slopes. But we must protect these places so that everyone can enjoy them in the future.

Jumping off

Hang-gliders jump off mountain tops to float down on their wings. They glide on the warm air that rises from the ground.

protect – *to look after and keep from harm*

Winter sports

Skiers and snowboarders love snow-covered mountains. They can slide and jump down the slippery slopes.

When the snow melts

Many tourists drop their rubbish on mountain visits. This pollutes the area and can harm the wildlife that lives there.

pollutes – *makes harmful waste that damages the environment*

Mountain resources

Hidden inside mountains lie valuable resources, such as building materials and metals. There are also useful resources on the slopes, such as trees.

Building blocks

Each day, big dumper trucks remove tonnes of rock and rubble from mountains. It is used to make buildings and bridges.

resources – *raw materials that can be used to make other things*

Cutting down trees

Logging companies plant fast-growing trees on mountainsides. When the trees are grown, loggers cut them down for timber and fuel.

Mining metal

Some mountain rocks are rich in gold, silver, copper and tin. Miners use large drills to dig these metals out of the stone.

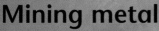

fuel – a substance used for producing heat or power by burning

Mountaineering today

Today's mountaineers are well prepared for their climbs. They have special food for energy, layers of clothing for warmth and lots of safety equipment.

A good night's rest

Mountaineers shelter in tents at night and in bad weather. The tents are light to carry, strong and waterproof.

safety equipment – ropes, harnesses and picks that are needed for climbing

Oxygen supply

Climbers carry tanks of oxygen, which they use to help them to breathe more easily in the thin mountain air.

Climbing suit

Climbers wear one-piece suits filled with down for warmth. The suit is windproof and waterproof.

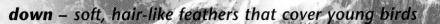

down – *soft, hair-like feathers that cover young birds*

Reaching the top

Mountain climbing is a popular sport. Many people have now climbed even the highest mountains, including the tallest on land, Mount Everest.

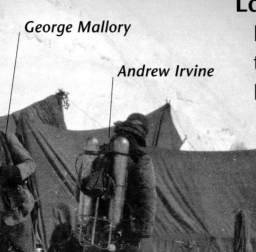

George Mallory

Andrew Irvine

Last climb

Mallory and Irvine began to climb Everest in 1924. Both men died on the mountain, but no one knows if they reached the top before they died.

Extraordinary climber

Reinhold Messner has climbed the world's 14 highest peaks. He is the first person to climb Everest without extra oxygen.

oxygen – *one of the gases in air*

Wonder woman

Catherine Destivelle is a world-class climber. She often tackles dangerous slopes and often uses only one or two of her fingers to pull herself upwards.

world-class – *among the best in the world*

Avalanche!

A large mass of snow and ice can suddenly break loose and crash down a mountainside. This is called an avalanche.

Predicting avalanches

Scientists use information gathered in weather stations like this one to help them predict when avalanches are likely.

predicting – *knowing that something is going to happen*

Avalanche in action

Some avalanches move as fast as a racing car. They sweep away everything in their path, including trees, people and even villages.

Protection

This steel fence has been built to stop an avalanche from reaching the town further downhill. It will slow down an avalanche.

steel – a strong metal made from iron and carbon

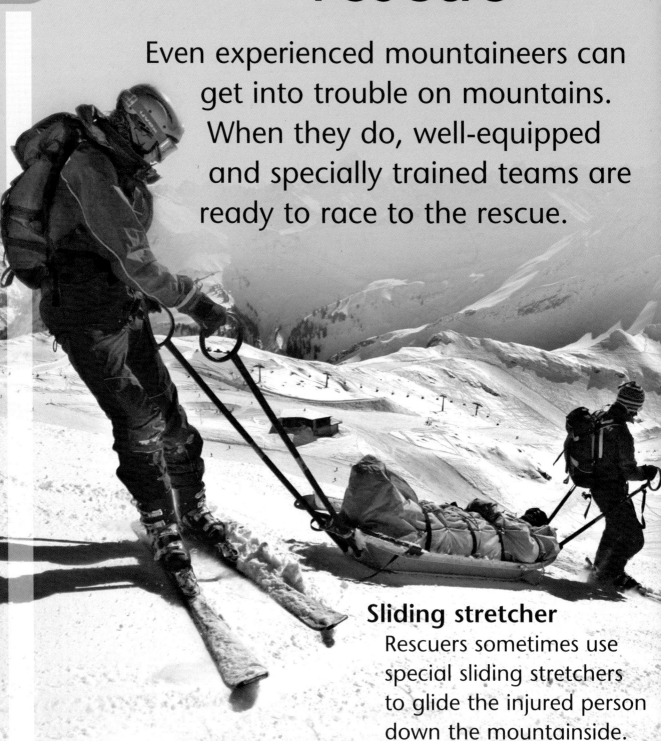

Mountain rescue

Even experienced mountaineers can get into trouble on mountains. When they do, well-equipped and specially trained teams are ready to race to the rescue.

Sliding stretcher
Rescuers sometimes use special sliding stretchers to glide the injured person down the mountainside.

experienced – *people who have skill which they have gained over time*

Helicopter rescue

Helicopters can reach remote peaks quickly. Rescuers can then help the injured people and take them to hospital.

Rescue dog

St Bernard dogs have a strong sense of smell. They can be specially trained to sniff out the victims of avalanches.

remote – out of the way places

Mountain mysteries

People sometimes see some strange things when they climb a mountain. They might find fossil fish, or they might be followed by a huge shadow.

Ghostly shadow

If someone climbs a mountain when the sun is low, the sun casts an enormous shadow on any low clouds.

fossil – the remains of ancient animals or plants found in rock

Something fishy

People often find fossil fish in rocks in fold mountains. Millions of years ago, these mountains were part of the seafloor.

Bigfoot

Some people believe a large creature called Bigfoot roams the Rocky mountains. No one knows if it really exists.

seafloor – the land at the bottom of the sea

Making mountains

Make a fold mountain range

Discover how land is forced upwards when two plates collide by doing this simple experiment.

1

Roll out each ball of clay to make a rough square 25mm thick.

You will need

- 2 balls of modelling clay, different colours
- Tray
- Rolling pin
- Plastic food wrap

2

Lay both pieces on the plastic food wrap on the tray 10mm apart.

Gently push the two clay blocks together. Your mountain range will rise upwards.

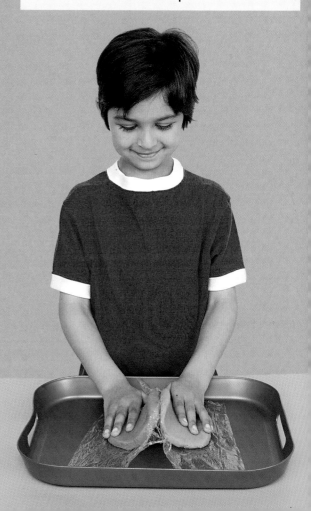

Leaving footprints

Bigfoot's calling card

Bigfoot's footprints are called its 'calling card'. Make one to give to a friend.

You will need
- Large sheet of card
- Paints and paintbrush
- Marker pen or felt-tip pen
- Scissors
- Sponge

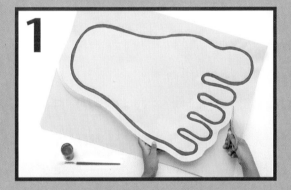

1

Fold the card in half, then paint a big foot shape. Cut out the shape, but do not cut the folded side.

2

On a sponge, draw a smaller foot shape. Cut this out.

3

Dip the sponge in some paint and decorate your card with lots of little footprints walking up towards the toes.

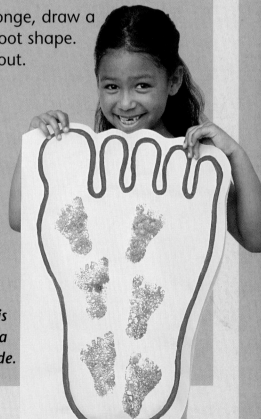

Your giant calling card is ready. Write a message inside.

Moving cable car

Make a cable car

Cable cars can climb high mountains on moving cables. Make a model with stations at the top and bottom of your mountain range.

You will need

- 3 small cereal boxes
- Coloured paper
- Sharp coloured pencil
- Modelling clay
- 1 long, 1 short piece of string
- Marbles
- Sticky tape
- 1 small sweet box

Cover the cereal boxes with coloured paper. Decorate with shapes of mountains and trees.

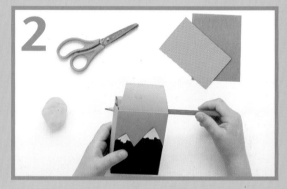

Pierce a hole in the top of each box with a sharp pencil. Use modelling clay to push against.

Thread the long piece of string through the holes as shown.

Place some marbles in each box, then tape the boxes shut.

5

Decorate the small sweet box with coloured paper to make it look like a cable car.

6

Tape the short piece of string to the car, then tie it to the middle of the long piece of string.

Place the top station on a box. By pulling on the long piece of string, you can move your cable car from the station at the bottom, up the mountain to the station at the top.

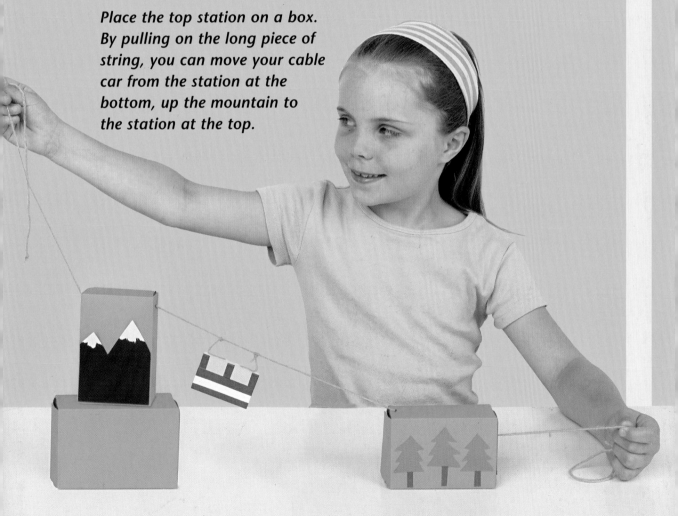

Index

air 7, 17, 35
animals 24–25, 26
avalanches 38–39, 41
Bigfoot 43, 45
birds 15
building materials 32
cable cars 29, 46–47
climbing 34–35, 36–37
crust 8, 9
earthquakes 9
farmers 26, 27
fault-block mountains 12
fold mountains 13, 44
footprints 45
fossils 43
glaciers 18–19, 21
ice 18–19, 20, 21, 38
lava 11
magma 10, 11
mining 33
mountain rescue 40–41

mountaineering 34–35, 36–37
mysteries 42–43
peaks 6, 7, 36
people 26–27
plants 14–15, 22–23
plates 8–9, 11, 12–13
rain 16
resources 32–33
roads 28
snow 7, 17, 18, 23, 31, 38–39
storms 15, 17
tourism 30–31
travel 28–29
trees 14–15, 22, 33
volcanoes 10–11, 24
weather 16–17, 22, 38
winds 15, 17, 20, 22, 24